British Cars of the Early Sixties 1960-1964

Compiled by David J. Voller

ISBN 0 85429 567 4

A **FOULIS** Motoring Book

First published, in the Auto Library Series, by Frederick Warne, 1981
Reprinted 1986 & 1989

Published by:
Haynes Publishing Group
Sparkford, Nr. Yeovil,
Somerset BA22 7JJ

Haynes Publications Inc,
861 Lawrence Drive, Newbury Park,
California 91320 USA.

Other titles in this series

The British motor industry at the start of the sixties comprised basically the 'Big Five' (BMC, Ford, Rootes, Standard-Triumph and Vauxhall) and numerous smaller manufacturers. Having survived the severe raw material and resource shortages of the immediate post war years and undergone a period of rebuilding and stabilisation in the 1950s, companies were seeking to produce attractive and reliable motor cars particularly for the vital and increasingly competitive world markets.

In the event, it was a testing time for large and small companies alike. Britain's failure to get into the Common Market was felt to be a great setback to the industry, particularly as the nation's export difficulties caused serious problems for a trade which needed to sell something approaching half its products overseas to survive. Rootes and Standard-Triumph, the two weaker companies of the Big Five, would probably have gone under had it not been for American backing and a merger with Leyland Motors, respectively. The worldwide resources of the Chrysler Corporation gave the Rootes Group a much needed boost and a tie-up between Leyland Motors and Standard-Triumph International emerged as the Leyland Motor Corporation which quickly became a competitive force particularly on the difficult American markets.

Despite the economic and production problems which beset the industry some superb motor cars were produced during the period covered by this book, not least the Mini, Cortina and 'E' Type which rapidly achieved universal recognition and soon became household names. The Ford Cortina in its first two years of operation built up sales faster than any vehicle since the Model T and BMC's advanced 1100 design became the most flatteringly plagiarised in Europe.

Manufacturers were generally still tending to concentrate on variety, although development patterns were beginning to emerge, notably from BMC, with their front-wheel drive Mini and 1100 ranges, and Triumph, with the Herald, Vitesse and Spitfire models.

The period will certainly be remembered by many enthusiasts as the age of the 'kit car'. A number of specialist companies produced, mainly for do-it-yourself home assembly, body and chassis packages which would accept engine/transmission units and suspension systems from established manufacturers, notably Ford and BMC.

A selection of the cars produced during the early sixties, some well known, others not so well known, is included in this book, the 27th title in the Olyslager Auto Library.

1960

Manufacturers entered the new decade somewhat optimistically having achieved a period of steady growth since the mid-fifties. An interesting collection of new models was introduced for the 1960 model year including the AC Greyhound, Aston Martin DB4 GT, Austin Seven, Ford Anglia 105E, Morris Mini, Sunbeam Alpine and Vanden Plas Princess 3 litre, together with a number of updated and facelifted vehicles. A total of 1,352,728 cars was produced during the year, of which 777,411 were sold on the home market and 573,317 (representing 42·5% of the total) were exported. The value of these export car sales was in excess of £225 million. Sadly during the year economic pressures saw the closure of a famous manufacturer, namely Armstrong Siddeley, who had been producing quality motor cars since 1919, and also Berkeley who had been fighting to establish themselves in the small sports car market for a number of years. A notable landmark was achieved during the year when Morris Minor number 1,000,000 rolled off the assembly line.

4A AC Greyhound

4B Armstrong Siddeley Star Sapphire 6

4A: **AC** Greyhound, introduced in October 1959, was a two-door, four-seater, 'grand touring' sports saloon powered by the high performance, Bristol D2, six-cylinder, 1971-cc, ohv, 105-bhp engine. The aluminium body was mounted on a rigid tubular steel chassis, although extensive use was made of fibreglass in a number of areas, including the bulkhead, rear seat pan and rear wheel arches. The Greyhound was distinguishable from the two-seater hard-top Aceca, which continued in production along with the open two-seater Ace, by its knife-edge nose, angular headlamp recesses and bonnet air scoop. Quantity production began to get under way in November 1960, by which time the model, as shown, had a wrap-around rear window, narrower radiator grille with four horizontal bars and fog lamps located outside the grille. The unique braking system featured twin hydraulic circuits with discs at the front and drums at the rear.

4B: **Armstrong Siddeley** Star Sapphire 6 Light Saloon, announced in October 1958 and continued unchanged, was the last but one model to come from this famous company, which due to inevitable economic pressures ceased production in the summer of 1960 after more than forty years as a motor manufacturer. The last model to be introduced was the luxuriously appointed, seven-seater limousine, also fitted with a six-cylinder, 3990-cc, ohv power unit; its top speed of 90 mph was less than for the saloon as it was considered inappropriate for a sedan of this distinction to exceed such a figure!

5A: **Aston Martin** DB4 GT, Sports Coupé, introduced in September 1959, and its DB4 saloon counterpart, introduced the previous year, formed the company's model range at the outset of the decade. Powered by a six-cylinder, 3670-cc, twin ohc engine which developed 302 bhp at 6000 rpm, the GT featured disc brakes all round, a limited-slip differential, 30 gallon fuel tank, front hinged bonnet and faired-in headlamps and was some five inches shorter than the saloon at 14 ft 3⅜ in. Price £4534 (£3755 for the saloon).

5B: **Austin** Seven was introduced at the Earls Court Motor Show in October 1959. A companion model to the Morris Mini-Minor, which had taken the motoring world by storm some two months earlier, it was distinguishable by the radiator grille, which had twelve straight vertical chrome and nine 'wavy' horizontal bars, and its 'Se7en' badges; the models soon became universally billed the 'Mini range'. The brainchild of designer Alec Issigonis, this two-door, four-seater was available in basic and de luxe form and fitted with a transversely-mounted, four-cylinder, 848-cc ohv, front-wheel drive engine and all-independent springing by rubber cones. Price was £496 (basic) and £537 (de luxe).

5C: **Austin** A40 Farina Countryman was introduced in September 1959. Generally identical to the saloon version announced in the summer of 1958, except for the fully opening rear end comprising a top-hinged window and let-down boot lid, this popular family car was powered by the BMC four-cylinder, 948-cc, ohv engine unit, which developed 34 bhp at 4800 rpm. Available in basic and de luxe form.

5A Aston Martin DB4 GT

5B Austin Seven

5C Austin A40 Farina Countryman

6A Austin A99 Westminster

6B Austin-Healey 3000

6C Bentley Series 'S'

6A: **Austin** A99 Westminster Saloon, introduced in July 1959, was continued with a number of improvements including a new steering gear, modified rear bumper and revised seat cushions. The power unit was the BMC six-cylinder, 2912-cc, ohv, 108-bhp engine with either a three-speed gearbox with overdrive or automatic transmission. This model was discontinued in September 1961 with the introduction of the A110 Westminster.

6B: **Austin-Healey** 3000, introduced in March 1959, was continued with minor modifications. Available in two-seater or two/four-seater form, this powerful sports car was similar in appearance to the 100 Six, which was in production between 1956 and 1959.

6C: **Bentley** Series 'S' was introduced in S2 form in the summer of 1959. Powered by the company's new V8, 6230-cc, ohv engine the S2 included power-assisted steering and a dual hydraulic braking system as standard, and was available in four basic forms: a four-door, all-steel saloon (shown), drophead coupé by H. J. Mulliner, and special long-wheelbase versions by James Young and Park Ward. Full air-conditioning was a standard feature of these superb cars. Prices ranged from £5660 to £8942.

7A Berkeley B 95

7B Bristol 406

7C Citroën Bijou

7A: **Berkeley** two-seater sports. The company started the year with a four-model range (B 95, QB 95, B 105, QB 105) comprising open and hardtop models in two body sizes. Powered by a two-cylinder, 692-cc, ohv engine driving the front wheels (standard and high performance versions available), the range was distinguishable from the three-cylinder, two-stroke engined range which it replaced, and the two-cylinder two-stroke engined model (reintroduced with a four-speed gearbox in the summer of 1960) by a square grille with horizontal bars and modified front wings and bonnet. All Berkeley production ceased in December 1960.

7B: **Bristol** 2·2 litre, 406 Saloon, first introduced in August 1958 (406E, the export version in October 1957), was continued with a number of changes including a revised grille featuring a mesh design in place of vertical slats, fog lamps located behind the bumper, and overriders as standard. The six-cylinder, 2216-cc, ohv engine, which developed 105 bhp at 4700 rpm, gave the car impressive acceleration and a top speed of at least 100 mph in overdrive top. The body was aluminium panelled over an all-steel frame welded to a box-section chassis. Price £4244. An Italian bodied version, by Zagato, was also available.

7C: **Citroën** Bijou, announced in October 1959, was one of several British-built models from Citroën Cars Limited of Slough. Styled in Britain, this little two-door, four-seater saloon was based on the French 2CV and featured a two-cylinder, 425-cc, ohv engine driving the front wheels, and independent suspension all round. Production was discontinued in the summer of 1964.

8A Daimler Dart SP250

8B Daimler Majestic Major

8C Ford Popular 100E

8A: **Daimler** Dart SP250 Sports, originally announced with left hand drive for the export market in April 1959, was produced with right hand drive from October 1959 onwards. This model represented a break with tradition for Daimler whose name had always been synonymous with more formal and refined methods of transport. Powered by a V8, 2548-cc, ohv engine which developed 140 bhp at 4800 rpm, the Dart featured a fibreglass, two-door body with two front seats and an occasional rear bench seat, and a wide, low version of the traditional Daimler grille. Maximum speed was in the region of 120 mph. Price was very competitive at £1395.

8B: **Daimler** Majestic Major Saloon was announced in October 1959, although production did not commence until November 1960. It was similar to the Majestic Saloon (in production from 1958 to 1962) but featured a larger boot which extended beyond the rear wings, modified, wrap-around bumpers and a new 4·5-litre, V8 engine which developed 220 bhp at 5500 rpm and gave the vehicle an impressive 120 mph top speed.

8C: **Ford** Popular 100E De Luxe Saloon replaced the Popular 103E saloon in September 1959, the upright body of the earlier series being superseded by the full-width, flush-sided body of the Anglia 100E. The model was powered by a four-cylinder, 1172-cc, side-valve engine which developed 36 bhp at 4500 rpm. Distinguishable from the Prefect 107E primarily by its mesh radiator grille (as fitted to the Anglia 100E). The basic Popular was the lowest priced family saloon on the British market, at just over £494.

9A Ford Anglia 105E

9B Ford Prefect 107E

9A: **Ford** Anglia 105E Saloon, introduced in September 1959, marked a complete break with Dagenham tradition in the light car field, and quickly established itself as a best seller on the world markets. The sleek body styling, featuring a reverse-angle rear window, two wide opening doors and a large glass area, was complemented by notable mechanical advancements, including a compact, lightweight, high-revving four-cylinder, 997-cc, ohv engine which developed 39 bhp at 5000 rpm, a four-speed gearbox with synchromesh on the top three ratios and independent front suspension. Initially available in standard and de luxe saloon form, the latter being distinguishable by a full width radiator grille and better trim. An estate car version was added to the range in the summer/autumn of 1961.

9B: **Ford** Prefect 107E Saloon De Luxe replaced the Prefect 100E model in September 1959. Powered by the Anglia's four-cylinder, 997-cc, ohv engine, this four-door family model featured as standard a number of refinements normally only available as extras on a car of this class. Discontinued in March 1961.

9C: **Ford** Zephyr Estate Car. Consul, Zephyr and Zodiac models continued with no material changes. These popular cars were powered by either a four-cylinder 1703-cc, ohv (Consul only) or six-cylinder, 2553-cc, ohv engine (Zephyr and Zodiac only).

9C Ford Zephyr Estate Car

10A Frazer-Nash Continental

10B Gilbern Mark 1 Gran Turismo

10C Hillman Husky Estate Car Series II

10A: **Frazer-Nash** Continental Gran Turismo Coupé. The last model to come from this famous builder of classic hand-built performance cars, this elegant two-door, two-seater (announced in 1957) was powered by a V8, 3·2-litre, BMW engine, which developed 173 bhp at 5500 rpm, and featured a sleek light-alloy body. Maximum speed was in excess of 1·30 mph. A Sebring open two-seater was also available. Production discontinued the following year.

10B: **Gilbern** Mark 1 Gran Turismo. High performance sports saloon/coupé from this independent company whose special claim to fame was that of being the only Welsh-based motor manufacturer. Available initially in kit form, or complete to individual order only, these attractive vehicles featured a fibreglass body shell on a tubular chassis frame and were available with a choice of engine: BMC 948 cc, MG 1558 cc or Coventry Climax 1098 cc.

10C: **Hillman** Husky Estate Car Series II was introduced in March 1960 with a number of modifications including vertical bar grille styling, a larger windscreen and rear window, lower roof line with overhang and a close-ratio gearbox. Powered by a four-cylinder, 1390-cc, ohv engine which developed 51 bhp at 4400 rpm, this sturdy little utility vehicle was also given a hypoid rear axle, in place of the spiral bevel unit, in the summer of 1960 before being replaced by the Series III version in 1963.

10D: **Hillman** Minx Series IIIA (Saloon Special and De Luxe, Convertible and Estate Car versions offered) became available in September 1959 and differed from its predecessor (Series III) as a result of modifications which included five horizontal bars located in centre divide mesh grilles, rectangular side lamp units, a close-ratio gearbox, bigger and more powerful brakes (except the Special), small curved tail fins and a floor mounted gearchange as standard. Easidrive automatic transmission was also available as an option. The four-cylinder, 1494-cc, ohv power unit developed 50·2 bhp.

10D Hillman Minx Series IIIA

11A: **Humber** Hawk was continued and with Series IA specification (from October 1959) was distinguishable by means of full length body side-flashes and a band of horizontal pleating on the door trim. Gearbox modifications also introduced resulted in closer gear ratios. The Hawk, which was first introduced in 1957, was available in saloon, touring limousine and estate car versions and was powered by a four-cylinder, 2267-cc, ohv engine which developed 73 bhp at 4400 rpm. Similar in general appearance to the Super Snipe.

11B: **Humber** Super Snipe was introduced in Series II form in October 1959. Modifications included a larger engine (2965 cc), front disc brakes and body changes featuring tapered side flashes, name over grille and five horizontal bar grille styling. The six-cylinder, ohv, power unit developed 121 bhp at 4800 rpm. Available as a saloon, touring limousine and estate car.

11C Jaguar 2·4 Mark II

11C: **Jaguar** 2·4 Saloon Mark II was introduced in October 1959. First announced in 1956, this powerful sports saloon now featured disc brakes all round, improved visibility with slimmer pillars, modified centre grille rib, small faired-in side lamps on top of the wings, semi-recessed foglamps and a wider track rear axle. The six-cylinder, 2483-cc, twin ohc engine developed 120 bhp at 5750 rpm, giving the car a top speed in excess of 100 mph. 3·4 and 3·8 Saloons were also available and of similar appearance.

11A Humber Hawk

11D Jaguar XK150

11B Humber Super Snipe

11D: **Jaguar** XK150 3·8 litre was introduced in October 1959 as a companion model to the 3·4 litre version which was announced in 1957 and continued the earlier classic XK120 theme. Available as Fixed Head and Drop Head Coupé and Roadster versions, this powerful sports car was fitted with a six-cylinder, 3781-cc, ohc engine which developed 210 bhp in standard form and 250 bhp at 5500 rpm in 'S' form with high compression cylinder head and triple SU HD8 carburettors. Overdrive was standard on all models; limited slip differential and automatic transmission were optional. This model had a relatively short production run which ceased in 1961 as Jaguar were preparing to launch a dazzling newcomer on to the market.

12A MG MGA 1600 FH Coupé

12B MG Magnette Mk III

12A: **MG** MGA 1600, in Fixed Head Coupé and Sports Roadster form, was introduced in July 1959 as replacement for the earlier MGA which was powered by a 1489-cc engine and had been in production for almost four years. The '1600' engine was a four-cylinder, 1588-cc, ohv unit (dimensionally identical to the ohc unit fitted in the 1600 'Twin Cam' model discontinued in 1960) which developed 79·5 bhp at 5600 rpm and the car featured a number of modifications including restyled rear wing plinths and front disc brakes. Price was £1026 (FH Coupé), £940 (open Roadster).

12B: **MG** Magnette Mark III Saloon continued with modifications to the engine and a number of detail changes. First introduced in 1959 it shared the Farina body styling of the other medium range BMC saloons and was powered by the B-Series four-cylinder, 1489-cc, ohv engine, with twin-carburettors, which produced 66·5 bhp at 5200 rpm. This popular 'tuned' saloon featured a distinctive forward tilting MG grille and its interior was well equipped in relation to its price of just over £1000.

13A Metropolitan 1500 Series 4

13B Morgan Four-Four Series II

13C Morris Mini-Minor

13A: **Metropolitan** 1500 Series 4 Fixed Head Coupé and Convertible were reintroduced for the home market in the summer of 1960 after being restricted to export sales since replacing the Series 3 model approximately eighteen months earlier. This colourful little car, powered by a four-cylinder, 1489-cc engine, was originally designed in the USA and from 1954 was built in Britain by Austin in conjunction with Fisher Ludlow. It was discontinued in the spring of 1961.

13B: **Morgan** Four-Four Series II Tourer and competition models were continued with a number of modifications which included a wider cockpit, narrower running boards and rear wings and flashing trafficators. Powered by a four-cylinder, 1172-cc, side-valve engine, the model was replaced by a Series III Tourer in the autumn of 1960.

13C: **Morris** Mini-Minor Saloon. Following its much heralded introduction in the summer of 1959, this top-selling little four-seater was continued with a number of changes including improved interior trim, padding each side of the instrument cluster, modified shock absorbers and improved window catches. Identical to the Austin Seven except for radiator grille design, badges and detail fittings.

13D: **Morris** Minor 1000 continued unchanged. Available in Saloon, Tourer and Traveller versions, these very popular two- and four-door cars were powered by a four-cylinder, 948-cc, ohv engine which developed 37 bhp at 4800 rpm and featured a four-speed gearbox, independent front suspension and rack and pinion steering. Shown is Morris Minor number 1,000,000 coming off the assembly line.

13D Morris Minor 1000

14A Riley 1·5

14B Riley 4/Sixty-Eight

14C Rolls-Royce Silver Cloud II

14D Rolls-Royce Phantom V Limousine

14A: **Riley** 1·5 Saloon was continued with a number of changes including interior hinges on the boot and bonnet, a full width parcel shelf and modifications to the four-cylinder, 1489-cc, ohv engine which now produced 63·5 bhp at 5000 rpm. Price was £815.

14B: **Riley** 4/Sixty Eight Saloon was continued with engine modifications and detail changes. Powered by a twin-carburettor version of the BMC 'B' Series, 1489-cc engine, this car was of similar general appearance to the other medium range BMC Farina saloons but featured traditional Riley grille and badges, burr walnut veneer on the instrument panel and door cappings, full instrumentation and thick pile carpets. Price was £1028.

14C: **Rolls-Royce** Silver Cloud was now designated 'Silver Cloud II' and featured a number of changes including a larger engine (V8, 6230-cc in place of six-cylinder 4887-cc) power-assisted steering as standard, revised facia and the heating, demisting and air cooling units located under the front wings. Available in standard and long wheelbase versions and with alternative saloon, convertible and limousine coachbuilt bodies from James Young, H. J. Mulliner and Park Ward. The Rolls-Royce bodied, four-door saloon was priced at £5802.

14D: **Rolls-Royce** Phantom V Limousine was introduced in the summer of 1959. A long wheelbase, luxuriously equipped vehicle, which was mechanically similar to the Silver Cloud and Bentley Series 'S' models, it was available in a number of styles including seven-seater versions from James Young and Park Ward and touring models from James Young and H. J. Mulliner.

15A Rover 80

15B Rover 3 litre

15C Singer Gazelle Series IIIA

15D Standard 10 Companion

15A: **Rover** 80 Saloon was introduced in the summer of 1959 as a replacement for the 75 Saloon which had been in production for approximately ten years. Bodily similar to its predecessor, the new model featured a four-cylinder, 2286-cc, ohv engine which developed 77 bhp at 4250 rpm, overdrive, servo-assisted front disc brakes as standard, and a combined starter/ignition switch. A number of changes were made during the year. Also available was the larger engined 100 Saloon.

15B: **Rover** 3 litre Saloon continued with a number of changes including modified body trim and seating. Subsequent revisions were also made to the fresh air controls, window surrounds and roof guttering. Available with either manual or automatic transmission, this big five-seater was powered by a six-cylinder, 2995-cc engine, located, together with the suspension and auxiliaries, in a forward sub-chassis which was combined with a steel body of unitary construction. Maximum speed was in excess of 100 mph.

15C: **Singer** Gazelle Series IIIA Saloon was announced in September 1959. The four-cylinder, 1494-cc, ohv engine was now fitted with twin-carburettors, a special manifold, close-ratio gearbox, larger windscreen and headlamp cowls. Changes were also made to the body side flashes and rear light units. Convertible and estate car versions were also available.

15D: **Standard** 10 Companion. This sturdy little estate car was powered by a four-cylinder, 948-cc, ohv engine which developed 37 bhp at 4000 rpm and featured a four-speed gearbox. Overdrive and Standrive two-pedal transmission were optionally available.

1960

16A Sunbeam Rapier Series III

16B Sunbeam Alpine Sports

16C Triumph Herald

16A: **Sunbeam** Rapier. In Series III form, from September 1959, it featured a number of changes, including front disc brakes, a close ratio gearbox, larger windscreen, front side grilles with four instead of two narrow horizontal bars, narrower side flashes and a polished walnut facia with crash roll pad. The Rallymaster four-cylinder, 1494-cc, ohv power unit developed 78 bhp at 5400 rpm. Saloon and convertible versions were available, priced at £985 and £1042 respectively.

16B: **Sunbeam** Alpine Sports Tourer. Launched in the summer of 1959, this attractive two-door, two-seater (with occasional rear seats) was powered by an uprated 1½-litre Rapier engine which developed 83·5 bhp at 5300 rpm, and fitted with a close ratio gearbox. The distinctive body styling featured a sloping bonnet, narrow oval grille with horizontal bars, and tail fins.

16C: **Triumph** Herald. A 'twin-carburettor' saloon became available early in the year, the 'single-carburettor' saloon and 'twin-carburettor' coupé versions having been launched in the spring of 1959. This popular light car featured Italian styled bodywork of advanced design, which included a front-hinged all enveloping bonnet, mounted on a separate double backbone chassis. The four-cylinder, 948-cc, ohv engine developed 34.5 bhp at 4800 rpm (45 bhp at 5800 rpm with twin-carburettors). A convertible version was also added to the range—initially for export only.

16D: **Triumph** TR3A was continued with only minor changes. Originally introduced in 1957 for export only, it was later also sold on the UK market. Roadster and hard-top coupé versions were available, and the four-cylinder, 1991-cc, ohv engine which developed 100 bhp at 5000 rpm gave the car true sports car performance. The two-door body was classically Triumph with squared-off styling, a wide narrow grille and faired-in headlamps.

16D Triumph TR3A

17A Vanden Plas Princess 3 litre

17B Vauxhall Victor Super

17C Wolseley 1500

17A: **Vanden Plas** Princess 3 litre. Based mechanically on the Austin A99 and Wolseley 6/99, this six-cylinder engined luxury saloon was first introduced in the autumn of 1959 as the 'Princess', but given the Vanden Plas prefix in the spring of 1960. Manual and automatic transmission versions were available, priced at £1396 and £1467 respectively. A 4-litre long-wheelbase saloon and a limousine were also available.

17B: **Vauxhall** Victor F Series II Saloon was continued in various forms—an estate car was also available. Powered by a four-cylinder, 1508-cc, ohv engine this angular bodied model featured wrap around front and rear screens and a full-width radiator grille. Modifications made in August 1960 included chrome cappings on headlamp cowls (except standard versions) deeper rear window and full length side flutes.

17C: **Wolseley** 1500 Saloon continued with a number of changes including extended chrome side mouldings, interior hinges for bonnet and boot and full-width parcel shelf. Available in 'Family' and 'Fleet' versions this less powerful stable mate of the Riley 1·5 was fitted with a single-carburettor version of the 'B' Series engine which developed 50 bhp at 4200 rpm.

1961

1961

The year brought an abrupt downturn in fortunes, which resulted in a drop of approximately £100 million on export car sales. A total of 1,003,967 cars was produced by the U.K. industry, 602,174 of which were sold on the home market and 401,793 (representing 40·4%) went for export. New models introduced during the year included the Ford Consul Classic, Reliant Sabre 4, Triumph TR4, Jaguar 'E' Type and the Lea-Francis Leaf-Lynx. These last two mentioned vehicles were truly at opposite ends of the success spectrum. The 'E' Type, surely the most beautiful car of its type ever made, achieved tremendous popularity worldwide, whereas the Leaf-Lynx, which was to herald the return of Lea Francis to the world of car manufacturing, never reached production and only a few prototypes were made before the venture was scrapped. Regrettably Frazer-Nash ceased operating during the year.

18A: **AC** 2·6 Ace was not announced until the autumn of 1961, although production had started in March of that year. Powered by a Ford six-cylinder, 2553-cc, ohv engine, this classic two-seater sports model was distinguishable from contemporary AC- and Bristol-engined Ace's by its smaller radiator grille and lower bonnet line. Aceca hardtop version was also available.

18B: **Alvis** 3-litre Series TD21 Saloon. Introduced in 1958 this elegantly stylish car was continued with detail changes including larger sidelamps and quarter lights with chrome surrounds. Powered by a six-cylinder, 2993-cc, ohv engine which developed 124 bhp at 4000 rpm, the car featured bodywork by Park Ward. Wire wheels were optional. Drophead Coupé version was also available.

18C: **Aston Martin** DB4 GT Zagato. Impressive two-seater coupé body designed and constructed by Zagato in Milan and mounted on the DB4 GT chassis. The engine output of 302 bhp at 6000 rpm and the car's overall light weight gave it superb performance.

18A AC 2·6 Ace

18B Alvis 3 litre TD 21

18C Aston Martin DB4 GT Zagato

19A Austin Seven Countryman

19B Austin A55 Mk II Countryman

19C Austin-Healey Sprite Mk II

19A: Austin Seven Countryman. Nine inches longer than the saloon, this half-timbered estate car, announced in September 1960, featured an extended tail enclosing luggage space of $35\frac{1}{2}$ cu ft with the rear seat folded down. Loading doors were hinged vertically and the de luxe specifications included wing mirrors, heater and wheel discs as standard. Price £623.

19B: Austin A55 Mk II Cambridge Countryman. All steel bodied 'Farina' style estate car with the same dimensions as the saloon which was continued unchanged. The range was superseded by the Cambridge A60 in the autumn of 1961.

19C: Austin-Healey Sprite Mk II Sports replaced the Mk I 'Frog eye' in the spring. Although retaining the four-cylinder, 948-cc, ohv engine, albeit with a number of modifications which gave increased power output, it featured a new rectangular, squared-up body with conventionally positioned headlamps, rectangular mesh radiator grille and opening boot lid. Top speed was in the region of 85—90 mph and average fuel consumption an impressive 35—40 mpg.

19D: Austin-Healey 3000 Mk II Sports differed from the superseded Mk I mainly by a restyled radiator grille and modifications to the engine, including a new camshaft, stronger valve springs, and the adoption of triple carburettors, which increased the power output to 130 bhp at 4750 rpm. Top speed of this two/four-seater was an impressive 120 mph plus; however, limited ground-clearance restricted its manoeuvrability.

19D Austin-Healey 3000 Mk II

1961

20A/B: **Bentley** Continental and Series 'S' models continued unchanged. Shown are impressive examples of the beautiful Mulliner Continental and Park Ward Continental drophead coupés. Continental models were powered by the lightweight V8 engine used in the Series 'S', but featured lighter bodywork, higher gearing and other detail differences.

20C: **Daimler** Dart SP250 Sports. The advent of the 'Spec. B.' modifications in the spring gave the car a strengthened fibreglass body structure and bumpers, adjustable steering column, petrol reserve unit and switch, screen washers and exhaust pipe finishers all as standard rather than optional extras. Price was £3995. Also available in bare chassis form for body fitment by approved firms.

20A Bentley Continental Drophead Coupé

20C Daimler Dart SP250

20B Bentley Continental

20D EB Debonair SI GT

20D: **EB** Debonair S1 GT. This two/four-seater from EB (Staffs.) Ltd was available in kit form with a choice of engines, including the Ford Classic 109E unit.

21A Ford Anglia 105E Estate

21C Ford Consul Classic 109E

21B Ford Consul '375' Convertible

21D Hillman Minx Series IIIB

21A: **Ford** Anglia 105E Estate. First produced in the summer although not officially announced until the autumn, this attractive version featured an upward opening tailgate sloping to a convex 'V' at waist level. Available in standard and de luxe forms priced at £671 and £691, respectively.

21.B: **Ford** Consul '375'. Modified version of this popular Mk II range, which comprised saloon, saloon de luxe, convertible and estate car and featured front disc brakes as standard, sealed beam headlamps and '375' badges on the standard as well as the de luxe version. Superseded by the Consul Mk III range in the spring of 1962.

21C: **Ford** Consul Classic 109E Saloon. Introduced in late spring, this much heralded, medium priced newcomer featured twin headlamps, reverse rake rear window as on the 105E Anglia, tail fins, a four-cylinder, 1340-cc, ohv, 56-bhp engine, and front disc brakes as standard. Available in standard and de luxe versions with two or four doors, this four/five seater had a top speed of approximately 80 mph. Automatic transmission was optional.

21D: **Hillman** Minx Series IIIB. Improvements over the IIIA, announced in the summer of 1960, included hypoid rear axle replacing spiral bevel, improved air filter, larger oil pump and modified front seat squab. Available in saloon de luxe, convertible and estate car versions, and as a standard saloon to replace the earlier saloon special.

1961

22A: **Humber** Hawk Series II. Superseded the Series IA in the summer of 1960 and featured front disc brakes as standard, increased interior space, improved suspension, gearbox and instrumentation. Available in saloon and touring limousine versions.

22B: **Humber** Super Snipe Series III. Replaced the Series II in October 1960 and distinguishable by twin headlamps, full width grille of horizontal bars, single side strips, modified front seat squab to give increased leg room for rear seat passengers. Featured power-assisted steering and front disc brakes.

22A Humber Hawk Series II

22B Humber Super Snipe Series III

22C Jaguar 'E' Type

22C: **Jaguar** 'E' Type. Announced in March 1961, for export only, and introduced on to the UK market in July, this outstanding sports car, available in two-door two-seater open (detachable hard-top optional) and fixed head coupé styling, featured sleek, simple body lines embracing faired-in headlamps, a low wide air intake and a louvred bonnet with 'power bulge'. The 3·8-litre engine with triple carburettors gave the car superb performance, developing 265 bhp at 5500 rpm and with a top speed of around 150 mph. Developed from the famous 'C' and 'D' type sports/racing cars, the 'E' Type incorporated many features derived from international competition.

23A Jensen 541 'S'

23B Lea-Francis Leaf-Lynx

23A: Jensen 541 'S'. Replacement for the 541R which was discontinued in the summer of 1960, this model featured numerous changes including increased body width, greater headroom and luggage space, automatic transmission and limited slip differential as standard, air scoop in centre of fluted bonnet, seat belts as standard and an even more luxurious interior. The engine was a 4-litre BMC unit which developed 135 bhp, and the body was fibreglass with the exception of aluminium-panelled doors. Price £3195, or £3096 with the special order manual transmission.

23B: Lea-Francis Leaf-Lynx, was to mark the return of an old established firm when it appeared at the 1960 Earls Court Motor Show, but only a few prototypes were ever made and the car never reached production. Occasional, four-seater roadster powered by a 2½-litre Ford engine modified to develop 107 bhp at 4500 rpm and featuring a four-speed synchromesh gearbox and disc brakes all round. The unusual 'torpedo' style bodywork was all-steel apart from aluminium doors, bonnet and boot lid.

23C: Lotus Elite Series II. Modified version of this very attractive two-seater, fixed head coupé, which was first launched by the brilliant Colin Chapman stable in the mid-fifties. Powered by a four-cylinder, 1216-cc, ohc engine which developed 75 bhp at 6100 rpm, or 83 bhp at 6500 rpm in the Special Equipment variant, which was introduced at the same time as the Series II Elite in October 1960.

23D: MG Midget. Revival of a famous marque name announced in the early summer. An alternative to the Austin-Healey Sprite, it shared the same body shell and mechanical specifications but was distinguishable by its radiator grille of vertical slats and MG badges. Price £689.

23C Lotus Elite Series II

23D MG Midget

24A MG MGA 1600Mk II

24B MG Magnette Mk IV

24C Morgan Plus 4 Super Sports

24A: MG MGA 1600 Mk II. Superseded the Mk I in the summer and changes included a larger engine—1622 cc, modified radiator grille of slats recessed between a sloping frame and a central bar, revised rear lamp clusters, Mk II motifs and leather cloth facia covering. Sports, roadster and fixed head coupé versions available Shown is MG's Chief Designer with the 100,000th MGA.

24B: MG Magnette Mk IV. Introduced in the summer, this Farina saloon differed from the Mk III version by having a larger engine—1622 cc, developing 68 bhp at 5000 rpm, an anti-roll bar on the front suspension and stabilizer bar at the rear, modified exhaust system, and automatic transmission available as an option.

24C: Morgan Plus 4 Super Sports. Introduced in March this addition to the Plus 4 range was powered by a twin, double-choke, Weber carburettor version of the Triumph 1991-cc engine with a four branch exhaust system and wire wheels as standard.

25A Morris Oxford Farina Traveller

25B Reliant Sabre 4

25C Renault Dauphine—Gordini

25D Rover 100

25A: **Morris** Oxford Farina Series VI. Announced in the summer, these modified saloon and traveller versions featured a larger engine—1622 cc, a radiator grille of eight horizontal bars curved under the headlamps to embrace side/flasher lights, and, on the saloon, a lower rear wing line.

25B: **Reliant** Sabre 4. Launched in March for export only as the 'Sabra'. Billed as the Company's second four-wheel model (the first being the Sussita, built by Autocars Ltd of Haifa, Israel, in 1958) it featured an unusual fibreglass body on a conventional steel chassis and a Ford Consul, four-cylinder, 1703-cc, ohv engine which developed 73 bhp at 4400 rpm. The coachbuilt body, which was available with a soft-top or detachable hard-top, had a drooping snout and an oval mesh radiator grille, protected by massive overriders. Wire wheels were optionally available.

25C: **Renault** Dauphine—Gordini. UK assembly of this French designed model commenced at Acton, London in April. Popular four-door family saloon powered by a four-cylinder, 845-cc, ohv engine. Available with either a three-speed, all-synchromesh or four-speed gearbox.

25D: **Rover** 100 Saloon. Continued unchanged, but in common with the 80 model, now designated the Mk IV. Powered by a six-cylinder, 2625-cc, 104-bhp engine, this model had the bodyshell used on the earlier '90' which was discontinued in 1959.

26A Singer Gazelle Series IIIC Convertible

26B Singer Vogue

26C Standard Vanguard Six

26D Standard Vanguard Vignalle

26A: **Singer** Gazelle Series IIIC. Announced in July 1961, it was distinguishable from the superseded Series IIIB (first introduced in September 1960) by a larger engine— (1592 cc), '1600' motifs on front doors, larger warning lights and a heater fitted as standard. Ammeter and oil pressure gauge were optionally available.

26B: **Singer** Vogue Saloon. Introduced in July this new model was fitted with a body similar to but larger than the Gazelle, and was distinguishable mainly by its double headlamps with angled chromium framing strips and squarer radiator grille. The engine was a four-cylinder, 1592-cc, ohv unit, developing 66·25 bhp at 4800 rpm, and four-speed manual or three-speed automatic transmissions were offered. An estate car version became available during the following year.

26C: **Standard** Vanguard Six. Released by Standard-Triumph in the autumn of 1960, this new model was externally similar to the four-cylinder engined Vanguard, however, the interior was finished to a more luxurious specification and three- and four-speed manual and automatic transmissions were available. The six-cylinder, 1998-cc, ohv power unit developed 85 bhp at 4500 rpm and the car had a top speed of 90 mph. Saloon and estate car versions were available, priced at £1021 and £1134 respectively.

26D: **Standard** Vanguard Vignalle Saloon. Continued with a number of changes including recirculating ball steering, longer rear springs, flush fitting scuttle air intake, four-speed gearbox with central gearchange as standard (three-speed with column change to order). Phase III estate car also available. Both models were discontinued in the summer of 1961.

27A: **Sunbeam** Rapier Series IIIA. Saloon and Convertible models replaced the Series III versions in the spring. Now fitted with a four-cylinder, 1592-cc, ohv engine developing 80 bhp at 4500 rpm and also featuring detail interior changes, this model was priced at £1029 (Saloon) and £1087 (Convertible). Overdrive was optional. Shown are four Rapiers used by the Northumberland County Police.

27A Sunbeam Rapier Series IIIA

27B Sunbeam Alpine Series II

27B: **Sunbeam** Alpine Series II. Changes introduced in the summer of 1960 when it replaced the Series I model included a bored out 1592-cc version of the original engine which developed 85·5 bhp at 5000 rpm, minor transmission and suspension modifications, the introduction of disc brake shields and detail interior modifications. Top speed was in the region of 100 mph.

27C Triumph Herald 1200

27C: **Triumph** Herald 1200. Announced in April this larger engined version, available in saloon, coupé and convertible form, was distinguishable by '1200' insignia, walnut veneer facia, white rubber bumbers, revised seating and a heater as standard. The new 1147-cc, ohv engine developed 39 bhp at 4500 rpm. An estate car version was added to the range in May. A Herald 'S' model was introduced in February, but all other 1-litre versions were discontinued during the year.

28A Triumph TR4

28C Warwick GT

28D Watford Cheetah

28A: Triumph TR4. First produced in July this new sports roadster was initially released for export only. It featured square cut body styling by Michelotti, with headlamps set into a full width radiator, a four-cylinder, 2138-cc, ohv, 105-bhp engine and a four-speed, all-synchromesh gearbox.

28B: Vauxhall Velox PA. Given a larger engine (2651 cc), improved brakes, larger wheels and, as a facelift for 1961, detail styling changes, improved lights and a redesigned instrument panel. Cresta PA model featured the same improvements.

28B Vauxhall Velox PA

28C: Warwick GT Two Litre. Produced by Bernard Roger Developments Ltd of Slough, Bucks, this two-door, four-seater, high performance model was powered by the Triumph 1991-cc, TR3 engine and featured a polyester resin body reinforced with fibreglass. Interior finish and fittings were to a high standard.

28D: Watford Cheetah Sports was available in kit form from Watford Sports Cars Ltd. The fibreglass body was mounted on a ladder-type, tubular steel chassis and the vehicle was generally designed to accept Ford components.

1962

The industry shook off the production problems of the previous year and export sales quickly climbed back to something near the level achieved in 1960. Car production for the year was 1,249,426, home sales accounting for 698,393 and export sales 551,033, representing 44·1% of this total. An impressive crop of new models appeared during the year including the Aston Martin DB4 Vantage Saloon, Bristol 407, Ford Consul Cortina, Ford Consul Capri Coupé, Jaguar Mk X, Lagonda Rapide, Morris 1100 and Triumph Vitesse. Variants on the 'Mini' theme were introduced by BMC in the form of the Austin Seven Cooper, Riley Elf and Wolseley Hornet.

29A: **Alvis** 3-litre TD21 Drophead Coupé. Spring marked the arrival of the Series II version of this impressive model. Changes included disc brakes all round, fog lamps recessed in round fresh air intakes each side of the radiator grille, vertical reversing lights flanking the number plate and other detail modifications. Series II saloon version available to similar specifications. Replaced by Series III, TE21 models in October 1963.

29B: **Aston Martin** DB4 Convertible. Introduced in the autumn of 1961 this model was slightly larger than the saloon and shared with it modifications such as a smaller bonnet air intake, restyled radiator grille, and the availability of an optional special series engine.

29A Alvis 3 litre TD21 Drophead Coupé

29B Aston Martin DB4 Convertible

29C: **Aston Martin** DB4 Vantage Saloon. March saw the introduction of this addition to the range, which featured faired-in headlamps, GT type facia and the Special series, high compression engine which developed 260 bhp at 5750 rpm. Price £3746.

29C Aston Martin DB4 Vantage

30A Austin Seven Cooper

30B Austin A40 Farina Mk II

30A: **Austin** Seven Cooper. Announced in September 1961 this high-performance addition to the range was fitted with a 997-cc, 55-bhp, twin-carburettor engine, three-branch exhaust system and remote control gear lever. Externally similar to the Super model except for eleven horizontal bar grille and badges. Morris Mini variant also available.

30B: **Austin** A40 Farina Mk II Saloon. Released in September 1961, it was clearly distinguishable from the superseded Mk I version by a seven horizontal bar radiator grille, winding windows, restyled facia with enclosed glove box, and folding rear seat squab as standard. The wheelbase was increased by four inches, an anti-roll bar was added to the front suspension and a change of carburettor increased the power output of the engine to 37 bhp. The Countryman version was similarly modified.

30C: **Austin** A60 Cambridge Saloon. Replaced the A55 Mk II Farina in the autumn of 1961. The modified body included lowered rear wings, a central horizontal bar on the radiator grille, restyled lamp clusters and coloured, curved side flashes. The four-cylinder, 1622-cc, ohv engine developed 61 bhp at 4500 rpm. The Countryman version was some three inches longer. New rear springs were fitted to the saloon during the summer. Diesel engined versions were also available.

30D: **Austin** A110 Westminster Saloon. Replaced the A99 in the autumn of 1961. With a two inch longer wheelbase than the A99, this top model in the Austin range featured improved rear seating, more luxurious interior, increased power from the 2912-cc engine and twin exhausts. Externally it was distinguishable by a restyled front with an eight horizontal bar radiator grille. Power steering and air conditioning became optionally available in July.

30C Austin A60 Cambridge

30D Austin A110 Westminster

31A Austin-Healey 3000

31B Bentley Series 'S'

31A: **Austin-Healey** 3000 Sports Convertible. First produced in the spring but not announced until the summer, this two/four seater addition to the range included a twin-carburettor version of the 3-litre power unit, shorter gear lever, curved windscreen, wind-up side windows, swivelling quarter lights and a redesigned hood with flexible rear window. The two existing 3000 Sports models were discontinued in June.

31B: **Bentley** Series 'S' models were modified at the start of the year when the heater system was improved, changes were made to the instrumentation and footrests were added for rear seat passengers. The model shown is a long wheelbase saloon with an electrically operated movable division between driver and passengers.

31C: **Bristol** 407 Saloon. Powerful two-door, 5·2-litre luxury sports saloon, bodily similar to the superseded 406 model, but the first Bristol model to be powered by a non-Bristol engine—a Canadian built Chrysler V8 unit. Independent front suspension was incorporated, the facia design was simplified and rear headroom increased. The side strips were also extended over the full length of the body. Price £5142.

31D: **Daimler** 4·5 litre. Eight-seater limousine added to the range during the autumn of 1961. Similar to the Majestic Major Saloon but had an increased wheelbase and was fitted with a sliding glass partition, two heating systems and power-assisted steering as standard. Maximum speed was in the region of 110 mph.

31C Bristol 407

31D Daimler 4·5 litre Limousine

32A: **Ford** Classic 116E Saloon. Replaced the 109E version during the summer. Featured a four-cylinder, 1498-cc, ohv engine which developed 59·5 bhp at 4600 rpm, and an all-synchromesh gearbox. All Classic production ceased in July 1963.

32B: **Ford** Consul Cortina 113E Saloon. First produced in the spring, although not officially announced until September, this new family saloon was the culmination of considerable investment and four years research and development by the Ford Motor Company. The two-door body was conventional compared with the ill-fated Classic and mechanical features included a four-cylinder, 1198-cc, ohv engine, all-synchromesh four-speed gearbox and drum brakes. It was priced at £639 in standard guise and £666 for the de luxe version. Four-door versions were introduced in October.

32C: **Ford** Consul Capri SB60 Fixed Head Coupé. Based on the American styling of the Ford Classic, this special two-door, two-seater was externally very similar to its four-door stable companion below waist level, but featured a coupé top with a low roof line, unframed side windows and a streamlined rear window. Powered by the 1340-cc, 54-bhp engine (replaced in July by the 1498-cc unit) available with either floor or column gear-change.

32A Ford Classic 116E

32B Ford Consul Cortina 113E

32C Ford Consul Capri

32D Ford Zephyr 4 Mk III

32E Ford Zephyr 6 Mk III

32D: **Ford** Zephyr 4 Mk III Saloon. Replaced the Mk II in the spring. Featured a restyled four-door body shell with an oblong radiator grille of concave vertical bars, and curved glass to all windows. Mechanical modifications included an all-synchromesh four-speed gearbox. Powered by the four-cylinder, 1703-cc engine of the earlier Consul. Changes introduced in the autumn included improved interior trim and increased rear seat space.

32E: **Ford** Zephyr 6 Mk III Saloon. Powered by a 2553-cc engine. Styling changes included a full-width, divided, oblong radiator grille incorporating single headlamps.

33A Fairthorpe Electron

33A: **Fairthorpe** Electron. New version of this two-seater open sports car announced by the Buckinghamshire based manufacturer in the autumn of 1961. Available with a Coventry Climax 1098-cc or 1220-cc engine, this model was lighter than its predecessor. The front end of the plastic body was designed to fit the less expensive Electron Minor as well, which continued in production either complete or in kit form. Zeta, Electrina and, latterly, Rockette models were also available.

33B: **Hillman** Minx Series IIIC. Replaced the Series IIIB during the summer of 1961. Changes included a larger engine, '1600' motifs, rounded bumpers and single side mouldings (saloon only). Saloon de luxe, convertible and estate versions available.

33B Hillman Minx Series IIIC

33C Hillman Super Minx

33C: **Hillman** Super Minx Saloon. Added to the range in October 1961, this new model had a larger body than the Minx featuring a full width radiator grille flanked by single headlamps and hooded wrap-around front and rear screens and small tail fins. Engine power was from the Rootes 1592-cc unit. Estate and convertible versions also introduced during the year.

33D: **Humber** Super Snipe Series IV. Distinguishable from the Series III, which it replaced in the summer of 1961, by a restyled rear window, central radiator grille badge and chrome finishing on roof guttering and tail fins. Various other changes also incorporated.

33D Humber Super Snipe Series IV

34A Jaguar Mk X

34A: Jaguar Mk X 3·8-litre Saloon. New four-door model of advanced design which received considerable praise when unveiled at the 1961 Earls Court Show. Lower, longer and wider than the Mk IX, it was powered by the E-type engine, featured E-type rear independent suspension and was distinguishable by a sloping bonnet line with a square radiator grille and dual headlamps.

34B Jaguar E-Type FH Coupé

34B: Jaguar E-Type 3·8-litre FH Coupé. Continued unchanged, together with the open two-seater, except for modifications to increase leg room.

34C: Lagonda Rapide Saloon. Announced at the Paris Motor Show in the summer of 1961, this sophisticated four-door, automatic saloon was the result of a design and development programme which started when Lagonda's only available models in 1958 (3-litre saloon and coupé) were discontinued. Powered by an enlarged version of the Aston Martin DB4's six-cylinder engine, the new car featured a UK-built body styled by Superleggera of Italy. Production was very limited and only 55 had been built when the model was discontinued in 1964.

34C Lagonda Rapide

34D Lotus Seven

34D: Lotus Seven. Available complete or in kit form, this light-weight machine had a choice of engine— Ford, BMC or Coventry Climax. Featured a tubular space frame, with panels of light alloy and cowlings in fibreglass. Price in kit form £499 basic.

35A: **MG** MGB Series GHN 3 Roadster. Announced in July as replacement for the popular MGA. This new sports car was entirely different from its predecessor and featured a two-door body with a high rear wing line, a large flat boot and a wide, shallow rectangular radiator grille. Powered by a modified B-Series 1798-cc engine developing 95 bhp at 5400 rpm, this popular vehicle had a top speed of around 105 mph.

35A MG MGB

35B Morris 1100

35B: **Morris** 1100 Saloon. The ADO 16 project, as it was known in BMC, emerged as an attractive family saloon, which was based on the Issigonis Mini principle and featured front wheel drive, a transversely-mounted, 1098-cc power unit combined with transmission and final drive, and inter-connected rubber/hydraulic (Hydrolastic) suspension. Available in two-door (initially for export only) and four-door versions. The mechanical layout and revolutionary suspension gave the car exceptional passenger space and road holding as well as a comfortable ride. Shown with the 1100 is Lord Nuffield.

35C Reliant Sabre GT

35D Reliant Sabre GT

35C/D: **Reliant** Sabre GT. First produced in June although not officially announced until the autumn, this fixed head coupé version featured a sloping roof line and modified rear end which resulted in increased luggage space and two occasional rear seats. This car was two inches longer than the open sports model.

36A: **Riley** Elf Saloon. Introduced at the 1961 Earls Court Show, this Mini variant differed from the basic versions in having an extended boot with tail fins and a traditional Riley grille at the modified front end. The most expensive Mini variant, it featured a wood veneer facia and other interior refinements.

36B: **Riley** 1·5 Saloon. The R/HS2 Series was distinguishable from the R/HS1 Series, which it replaced in the autumn of 1961, by a modified front end and round front side-lamp units. Head and leg room was increased and changes were made to the front seats.

36C: **Riley** 4/72 Saloon. Announced in September 1961 this model differed from the 4/68 Saloon (discontinued in October 1961) by having a larger engine—1622-cc, improved suspension and exhaust system and various detail changes. New rear springs were introduced in the following June.

36A Riley Elf

36B Riley 1·5

36C Riley 4/72

37A Rochdale Olympic

37B Rover 95

37C Rover 3-litre Coupé

37A: **Rochdale** Olympic was produced by the Lancashire-based Rochdale Motor Panels company, either in kit form or in a body/chassis unit to accept a variety of engines (including BMC 'A' Series, Ford 105E and Riley 1·5 litre) and a choice of suspension systems. The attractive body was fibreglass and the car's performance gave it a top speed of over 100 mph.

37B: **Rover** 95 Saloon. Introduced in July, this model was bodily similar to the superseded 80 Saloon. The engine was a six-cylinder, 2625-cc unit which developed 102 bhp at 4750 rpm. Overdrive was not available. Discontinued in the summer of 1964.

37C: **Rover** 3-litre P5. The Mk IA Saloon was introduced in the summer of 1961, with detail changes, such as new wheel trims and quarter lights, only to be superseded in the following July by the Mk II which incorporated various modifications including a close ratio gearbox and increased engine power. The Fixed Head Coupé shown was also introduced in July and was distinguishable by a lower roof line.

37D: **Singer** Vogue Estate. Announced in May, this variant was dimensionally similar to the saloon. Both models were superseded by Mark II versions in August.

37D Singer Vogue Estate

38A Standard Ensign De Luxe Estate Car

38A: **Standard** Ensign De Luxe Estate Car. Introduced early in the year this variant and its saloon counterpart had a larger engine than the standard Ensign Saloon, which was discontinued the previous summer, a four-speed gearbox, improved trim and fittings and modified instrumentation. Both versions were discontinued in the following spring.

38B: **Sunbeam** Alpine Harrington Le Mans. This specialist conversion of the popular Alpine sports model was available from the autumn of 1961.

38B Sunbeam Alpine Harrington Le Mans

38C Triumph Vitesse

38C: **Triumph** Vitesse. Available in saloon and convertible form this model was based on the Herald specification which included an all-enveloping, front-hinged bonnet and a 25-foot turning circle. Visible differences included front flared wings over diagonal twin headlamps, an oblong mesh grille, aluminium bumpers and special wheel trims. Power was from a six-cylinder, 1596-cc, ohv engine which developed 70 bhp at 5000 rpm.

38D: **Triumph** TR4 Coupé. Announced in November 1961 this version had a detachable steel roof panel, which when removed left the rear screen and wind-up side windows in position.

38D Triumph TR4

39A Vauxhall Victor FB

39C Wolseley Hornet

39A: **Vauxhall** Victor FB Saloon. Successor to the F Series II in the summer of 1961, this new marque was distinguishable by lower body styling which featured sloping windscreen pillars, smooth body sides topped by a knife-edge moulding and a full-width radiator grille embodying single headlamps. The four-cylinder, 1508-cc engine was basically unchanged from the previous model.

39B: **Vauxhall** VX4/90 Saloon. Introduced with the Victor FB this more luxurious alternative was recognisable mainly by body side flashes, larger wheels, different wheel trims and radiator grille. The 1508-cc engine produced more power than the Victor FB (71·3 bhp instead of 48·5 bhp) and there were a number of other differences.

39C: **Wolseley** Hornet Saloon. Introduced in the autumn of 1961 this 'up-market' Mini variant was similar to the Riley Elf but was immediately recognisable by the illuminated name badge mounted on the grille.

39D: **Wolseley** 16/60 Saloon. Succeeded the 15/60 in the summer of 1961 and was distinguishable by front end changes, reduced rear fins and modified side mouldings. A larger engine (1622-cc), front suspension modifications and a new exhaust system were also featured.

39B Vauxhall VX4/90

39D Wolseley 16/60

1963

Total production for the year reached an impressive 1,607,939 cars, with 958,766 going to the home market and 649,173 of this total to export (representing 40%). The value of the export sales was approaching £250 million. Interesting newcomers to appear in the showrooms during the year included the Bond Equipe GT, Daimler 2·5 litre Saloon, Ford Consul Cortina Lotus, Hillman Imp, Humber Sceptre, Jensen C-V8 and Triumph Spitfire Sports.

40B Austin Mini Cooper 'S'

40A Aston Martin 3·7 litre DB4

40A: **Aston Martin** 3·7-litre DB4. The saloon and convertible continued with a number of changes including a higher wing line, increased rear passenger headroom, a larger boot, GT type facia and detail engine modifications. A DB4 Vantage GT saloon was also introduced during the year.

40B: **Austin** Mini-Cooper 'S' Saloon. More powerful alternative to the Mini-Cooper introduced in March and fitted with a twin-carburettor, tuned 1071-cc engine which developed 68 bhp at 5000 rpm, and servo-assisted disc brakes. Extremely lively performance gave the car a top speed in the region of 95 mph and rapid acceleration. Price £695. BMC replaced the Super and De Luxe models in the autumn of 1962 with the single Super De Luxe, which featured an oval instrument panel and revised interior trim.

40C: **Austin** A40 Farina. Saloon and Countryman models continued with a number of changes including a larger engine (1098-cc) and modifications to the gearbox.

40C Austin A40 Farina

41A Austin A60 Cambridge

41B Austin-Healey Sprite

41C Bentley Series 'S'

41D Bentley Continental 'Flying Spur'

41A: **Austin** A60 Cambridge Saloon. Duotone body finish became available in the autumn of 1962; detail changes were also introduced. A60 Countryman also continued with detail modifications.

41B: **Austin-Healey** Sprite. The AN7 replaced the AN6 in the autumn of 1962. Numerous changes included a larger engine (1098-cc producing 55 bhp), Lockheed front disc brakes, modifications to the gearbox, improvements to the driving compartment and modified instrumentation. Wire wheels were optionally available.

41C: **Bentley** Series 'S' Saloon. Received a major facelift in October 1962 when the S2 was replaced by the S3. Changes included a lowered bonnet, bolder wings with recessed sidelamp units, twin headlamps, smaller overriders (UK only), revised seating and modifications to the engine and power steering. See also Rolls-Royce Silver Cloud III.

41D: **Bentley** Continental. The Series S3 superseded the S2 in October 1962. Changes included twin headlamps and modifications to the engine and power steering.

42A Bond Equipe GT

42A: **Bond** Equipe GT. Whilst continuing to produce economy cars for the three-wheeled market, Bond made their debut in the four-wheeled field with the launch of the Equipe in the spring. Based on Triumph parts, in particular the Herald, this 2+2 sports coupé featured a fibreglass shell bolted to the Herald chassis, the 1147-cc engine, Herald suspension and a Spitfire-based braking system.

42C Elva Courier Mk III

42B: **Daimler** 2·5 litre Series XDM2 Saloon. Introduced in October 1962, this model was bodily identical to the Jaguar Mk II except for the traditional fluted radiator grille and 'D' emblem on the wheel discs. Featured a V8, 2548 cc, ohv engine, automatic transmission and disc brakes all round.

42C: **Elva** Courier Mk III Now produced by Trojan Ltd of Croydon, Surrey, following the signing of an agreement with Frank Nichols, the creator of the Elva, this latest version was available either complete or in kit form and was powered by the MGA 1622-cc engine. The majority of earlier sales went to the American market.

42B Daimler 2·5 litre

43A Fairthorpe Rockette

43A: **Fairthorpe** Rockette. Introduced in the summer of 1962, this decidedly unusual addition to the Fairthorpe range was easily recognisable, was available complete or in kit form and was powered by the Triumph Vitesse, six-cylinder, 1596-cc engine. The central headlight was discontinued in the summer of 1963.

43B: **Falcon** 515. Attractive fibreglass bodied sports coupé from Falcon Shells of Epping, Essex who produced, during the late fifties and sixties, a variety of 'specials' in kit form which would accept Ford, Coventry Climax and MG engines. The body was designed by Brazilian Tom Rohonyi.

43B Falcon 515

44A Ford Anglia Super 123E

44A: **Ford** Anglia Super 123E Saloon. Announced in November 1962, this version was similar to the 105E model but had a larger engine (1198-cc), bigger brakes, chrome edged body flashes and an improved interior. Wheel trims and a heater were fitted as standard.

44B: **Ford** Consul Cortina Super 118E Saloon. A larger engined (1498-cc) variant which was introduced at the start of the year. It also featured bigger brakes, improved interior trim and body chrome strips and was available in two- and four-door versions with either floor or column change. Estate car and GT versions were also announced during the year.

44C: **Ford** Consul Cortina 118E Estate Car Super. Added to the range in March, this variant was available with either column or floor change and featured the mechanical specification and styling of the four-door super saloon but with exterior wood style panelling. Overall length was 14 ft 0½ in. 113E De Luxe version also available.

44B Ford Consul Cortina Super 118E

44C Ford Consul Cortina 118E Estate

45A Ford Consul Cortina Lotus

45A: **Ford** Consul Cortina Lotus 125E Saloon. Developed by Lotus this powerful, sporting model appeared at the beginning of the year and quickly established itself in the performance saloon car field. Powered by a Lotus-Cortina bored-out, 1558-cc, ohc engine which developed 105 bhp at 5500 rpm. Top speed was 105 mph and acceleration 0–50 mph in 7·5 secs.

45C Ford Zephyr 4 Mk III Estate

45D Ford Zodiac Mk III

45B Ford Consul Capri GT

45B: **Ford** Consul Capri GT Coupé. This uprated variant announced early in the year featured increased bhp, a Weber carburettor, improved interior trim and a GT badge at the rear end. Price £900.

45C: **Ford** Zephyr 4 Mk III Estate Car. Introduced in the autumn of 1962. Built by Abbott of Farnham, Surrey. Zephyr 6 and Zodiac versions also available.

45D: **Ford** Zodiac Mk III Saloon. Continued with a number of changes, including increased track and modifications to the rear bulkhead and wheel arches to give increased rear seat space. Zephyr 4 and 6 variants were similarly modified.

46A Ginetta G4 Sports

46B Hillman Imp

46C Humber Sceptre

46D Jensen C-V8

46A: **Ginetta** G4 Sports. Introduced in 1961, this attractive, fibreglass-bodied model succeeded the 'G3' of 1960. The G3 had marked Ginetta Cars Ltd's arrival as a serious car constructor following the earlier 'G1/G2' development work of the founders of the company, the four Walklett brothers of Suffolk. Available with a choice of engine/gearbox packages, more than 500 G4 models were produced between 1961 and 1969. Shown is Ivor Walklett at the wheel of a 'G4' in racing trim.

46B: **Hillman** Imp Saloon. The Rootes Group launched their new 'baby' on to the small family saloon market in the spring, hoping that it would achieve something of the Mini's considerable popularity. This unusual little car was powered by a rear-mounted, aluminium, four-cylinder, 875-cc, ohc engine. Accommodation was good in relation to the car's size, with a top-hinged rear window giving access to luggage space which could be increased by folding down the rear seat. Standard and de luxe versions were available, priced at £508 and £535, respectively.

46C: **Humber** Sceptre Saloon. Added to the Humber range at the start of the year and based on the Hillman Super Minx and Singer Vogue. Distinguishing features included a small radiator grille of vertical bars, twin headlamps, sidelamp units set in horizontal bar side grilles and rear fin mouldings forming a 'Vee' around the rear lamp clusters. The technical specification included a close ratio four-speed gearbox and servo-assisted front disc brakes.

46D: **Jensen** C-V8 Saloon. This high performance luxury model was unveiled in the autumn of 1962. Featured a fibreglass body similar to the 541 (discontinued in the summer) mounted on a tubular and boxed chassis, a Chrysler V8, 5916-cc, 305-bhp power unit, Torqueflite automatic transmission and disc brakes all round. Finish and interior appointments were to a very high standard. Top speed was 135 mph plus. Price £3392.

47A Lotus Elan

47C MG 1100

47B MG Midget

47A: **Lotus** Elan Convertible. This attractive two-seater made its debut in October 1962. Featured a fibreglass body mounted on a fabricated steel backbone chassis, hydraulically-operated, retractable headlamps, a twin-cam, 1498-cc, 100-bhp engine (later replaced by a new 1588-cc unit), all-synchromesh gearbox, independent suspension and disc brakes all round. The driving compartment was comfortable and very well appointed. Price £1499

47B: **MG** Midget Series GAN 2 Sports. Changes introduced in the autumn of 1962 included a larger engine (1098-cc), Lockheed front disc brakes as standard, modifications to the gearbox and carpets in place of rubber mats. Wire wheels were optionally available.

47C: **MG** 1100 Saloon. High performance version of the Morris 1100 announced in the autumn of 1961. Distinguishable by traditional square MG grille and available in four-door and two-door (export only) form, this popular variant featured a twin-carburettor, 52-bhp version of the 1098-cc engine and more refined interior appointments.

48A Morgan Plus 4 Super Sports

48C Morris Minor 1000 Traveller

48B Morris Mini-Minor Traveller

48D Ogle SX 1000

48A: **Morgan** Plus 4 Super Sports. Introduced in October 1962, this variant featured lower body styling with a reduced frontal area and was powered by a tuned version of the 2138-cc Triumph engine. The 1991-cc Triumph engine was optionally available.

48B: **Morris** Mini-Minor Traveller. All-metal version became available on the UK market in the autumn of 1962. Otherwise identical to the wood battened Traveller which, together with the various saloon variants, was continued with minor changes.

48C: **Morris** Minor 1000. This very popular little car continued in its various forms, saloon, traveller and convertible, with a number of significant mechanical changes. A larger engine was fitted (1098-cc, producing 48 bhp), modifications were made to the gearbox and larger front brakes were introduced.

48D: **Ogle** SX 1000. This pretty two-door GT coupé, by industrial designer David Ogle, was based mechanically on the 997 cc-engined Mini-Cooper. The body was resin-bonded fibreglass and the interior finish and fitting were to a luxury specification. Price £1070.

49A Reliant Sabre 6 Sports

49A: **Reliant** Sabre 6 Sports was launched in the autumn of 1962. Differences from the Sabre 4 included a six-cylinder, 2553-cc, ohv engine, shorter bonnet without an air scoop, a wider, mesh radiator grille with division bar, modified rear wheel arches and twin exhaust pipes. The Sabre 4 was given the Sabre 6 bonnet and grille during the spring. An FH Coupé GT version was introduced at the start of the year.

49B: **Riley** Elf Mk II Saloon. The beginning of the year saw the arrival of the modified Elf which differed from the discontinued Mk I mainly by having a larger engine (998-cc producing 38 bhp) and modified front brakes.

49B Riley Elf Mk II

49C Rolls-Royce Silver Cloud III Convertible

49D Rolls-Royce Phantom V Limousine

49C: **Rolls-Royce** Silver Cloud III. Distinguishable from the superseded II by major exterior changes such as a lowered bonnet, restyled wings, dual headlamps, modifications to the engine and power steering and the availability of individual front seats as standard.

49D: **Rolls-Royce** Phantom V Limousine continued with a number of changes, namely twin headlamps and modifications to the engine and power steering.

50A Rover 110

50A: Rover 110 Saloon. Announced in the summer of 1962 this model was generally similar to the discontinued 100 Saloon, but the output of the 2625-cc engine was higher.

50B: Rover 3 litre P5 Mk II Saloon replaced the Mk IA. Differences included increased power from the 2995-cc engine, a close ratio gearbox, improved seating and trim and detail changes. A fixed head coupé was also available featuring a lower roof line and power steering as standard.

50C Singer Vogue

50C: Singer Vogue Series II Saloon and Estate Car superseded the Series I versions. Differences included front disc brakes, twin reversing lamps, individual front seats and two-speed wipers. The bonnet chrome strip featured on the Mk I was not included.

50D: Sunbeam Alpine Series III Sports Tourer and GT Hardtop replaced Series II variants. Changes included servo-assisted brakes, fixed front quarter lights, a larger boot and twin fuel tanks in the rear wings. The GT hardtop had a walnut facia, hinged rear quarter lights, de luxe trim and a heater. A single carburettor replaced twin-carburettors later in the year.

50B Rover 3 litre

50D Sunbeam Alpine

51A: **Triumph** Herald 12/50 Saloon. Skylight variant similar to the 1200 but with a sunroof as standard, increased output from the 1147-cc engine and front disc brakes as standard.

51B: **Triumph** Spitfire 4 Sports. Developed from the Herald, this attractive two-seater featured a Michelotti styled steel body with a downswept, front-hinged, front end, a recessed radiator grille with central vertical bar, raised beading along the wings and a generous luggage boot. The twin-carburettor version of the 1147-cc engine developed 63 bhp at 5750 rpm and the technical specifications also included the Herald's all-independent suspension and gearbox. Price £730.

51C Vauxhall Cresta PB

51A Triumph Herald 12/50

51D Wolseley Hornet

51B Triumph Spitfire 4 Sports

51C: **Vauxhall** Cresta and Velox PB Saloons. Replacements for the PA models, these variants had body shells similar to the Victor FB and featured improved versions of the previous 2651-cc engine, gearbox and suspension. Top of the Vauxhall model range they were more roomy, lighter and slightly lower than their predecessors, with a longer wheelbase.

51D: **Wolseley** Hornet Mk II Saloon featured a larger engine than its Mk I predecessor (998-cc), modified front brakes and detail changes.

1964

1964 Production continued to increase and by the end of the year a total of 1,867,640 cars had been manufactured. For the first time ever home market sales comfortably topped the million mark at 1,161,886 and export sales accounted for 705,754, representing 37·8% of total production. New models unveiled during the year included the AC Cobra, Aston Martin DB5, Bristol 408, Ford Corsair, Gordon-Keeble GK 1, Jaguar 3·4 litre 'S', Morgan Plus Four Plus GT FH Coupé, Rover 2000, Triumph 2000 and Vauxhall Viva HA.

52A AC Cobra

52B Aston Martin DB5 Saloon

52A: **AC** Cobra, originally introduced on to the export market for 1963, became available in rhd form in the autumn. This powerful sports car originated from an approach to AC by American racing driver Carroll Shelby, and, following an intensive design and development period of a little over a year, the model went into production. Cars were built at Thames Ditton, UK and shipped to the USA to be fitted with engines and gearboxes. Early versions were powered by a Ford V8 4·2-litre engine; later versions by a V8, 4·7-litre unit.

52B/C: **Aston Martin** DB5 Sports Saloon and Convertible models replaced the DB4s. Powered by a six-cylinder, 3995-cc, 282-bhp engine matched with either a four- or five-speed gearbox (four-speed only available on earlier models) this attractive new model featured a sleek two-door body with faired in headlamps and electrically operated windows. Price £4248 (saloon) and £4635 (convertible).

52C Aston Martin DB5 Convertible

53A: Austin 1100 Saloon. Unveiled in the summer of 1963 this Longbridge-produced version of the Morris 1100 announced in the summer of 1962 was distinguishable mainly by its front grille of eight horizontal wavy bars and central badges front and rear. Available in two- and four-door versions with standard or de luxe trim.

53B: Austin A110 Westminster Mk II. Replaced the Mk I in the early spring. Featured a new four-speed gearbox, with overdrive available as an option rather than as standard, modified suspension, smaller wheels and self adjusting brakes. The standard version shown had an anodised aluminium mesh grille and bonnet scoop, vinyl upholstery and a simplified facia whereas the Super De Luxe had luxury fittings and featured the Mk I radiator grille.

53C: Austin-Healey Sprite Mk III superseded the Mk II during the early spring. New features included a curved windscreen, fully winding windows, hinged quarter lights, lockable doors with external press button handles, three-spoke steering wheel and revised facia layout and instrumentation.

53D: Austin-Healey 3000 Mk III. Replacement for the Mk II, this version featured engine modifications including greatly increased power output and different carburettors, servo-assisted brakes, a wood veneer facia and a central, console-mounted gear lever.

53A Austin 1100

53C Austin-Healey Sprite Mk III

53B Austin A110 Westminster Mk II

53D Austin-Healey 3000 Mk III

54A Bentley Series 'S'

54A: **Bentley** Series 'S'. Continued with detail changes, namely the introduction of 'B' monograms in raised headlamp fairing surfaces and an increase in the wheel rim width.

54B: **Bentley** Continental continued with similar modifications to the Bentley S Series. Shown is the H. J. Mulliner, Park Ward fixed head two-door saloon.

54C: **Bristol** 5·2 408 Saloon. This impressive model was some five inches shorter than the 407, which was discontinued in March and distinguishable by a second set of headlamps in a wider, horizontal-bar radiator grille, a lower and squarer roof line, additional brightwork and modified tail fins and sidelamp units.

54B Bentley Continental

54C Bristol 5·2 408

55A Elva Courier Mk IV

55C Ford Corsair GT

55B Ford Corsair

55D Ford Zephyr 4 Mk III

55A: Elva Courier Mk IV. This T-Type sports car was billed as the only 100-mph open two-seater in Europe with fully independent suspension selling in the UK for under £1000 tax paid. It featured a reinforced metal and fibreglass body mounted on a ladder-type chassis with a choice of either the Ford Cortina GT 1489-cc or MGB 1798-cc power units.

55B: Ford Corsair 120E Saloon. This attractive new five-seater was available in standard and de luxe form with either two or four doors and floor or column mounted gear change. Powered by a four-cylinder, 1498-cc, 59·5-bhp engine, the model had body lines similar to the Cortina but featured unusual front end styling in which the front wings were moulded to a point. Automatic transmission was optionally available.

55C: Ford Corsair GT (120GT) Saloon. Similar to the 120E Corsair but featuring engine differences which increased the bhp and general performance, bucket seats, and a central floor-mounted gear lever as standard. Available in two- and four-door versions.

55D: Ford Zephyr 4 Mk III Saloon and Estate Car continued with a number of changes including a lowered radiator grille and interior improvements to the facia, trim and door releases. Zephyr 6 and Zodiac versions also continued with a number of detail modifications.

56A Gordon-Keeble GK I

56A: Gordon-Keeble GK 1 Touring Saloon. An exciting new two-door, four-seater unveiled at the beginning of the year by this specialist company, which was based near Southampton and formed following a tie-up between John Gordon, Managing Director of Peerless Cars in the fifties, and designer Jim Keeble. Features included a fibreglass body styled by Bertone of Italy, a V8, 5·3-litre Chevrolet engine and luxury finish and fittings. Price was just £2798.

56B Hillman Husky Series III

56B: Hillman Husky Series III replaced the Series II in the summer of 1963. Innovations included a lower bonnet line, a modified radiator grille incorporating sidelamp units, redesigned facia with full-width parcel shelf and a number of technical improvements.

56C: Hillman Minx Series V Saloon De Luxe. Major changes made to this latest version of the Minx (replacement for the IIIC range) included a modified roof line, larger windscreen with a squarer surround, radiator grille of five horizontal bar design with central badge, modified rear lamp units, individual front seats and a redesigned facia. Automatic transmission was optionally available.

56C Hillman Minx Series V

57A Jaguar 3·4 litre 'S'

57A: **Jaguar** 3·4 litre 'S' Saloon. This new model was based on the standard 3·4 Saloon but included a number of the Mk X's features, such as a flatter roof line, longer rear end and independent rear suspension. Other innovations included a heavier radiator grille surround, cowls over the head and fog lamps and shallow section bumpers. A 3·8-litre 'S' saloon was also available.

57B: **Jensen** C-V8 Mk II Saloon. Distinguishable from the discontinued Mk I version mainly by the smooth boot lid, combined sidelamp units below the headlamps and the lockable button in place of the chrome handle on the bonnet. The 5·9-litre engine was replaced by a 6276-cc, 330-bhp unit early in the year.

57C: **Marcos** 1800 was introduced early in the year. The independent Marcos company (founded by Jem *Mar*sh in collaboration with Frank *Cos*tin) had astonished the motoring world in 1960 with the appearance of their high-performance GT—the main chassis structure being made of wood! This Volvo-engined '1800' variant also had a wooden chassis, on which was mounted a sleek body fitted with faired-in dual headlamp units.

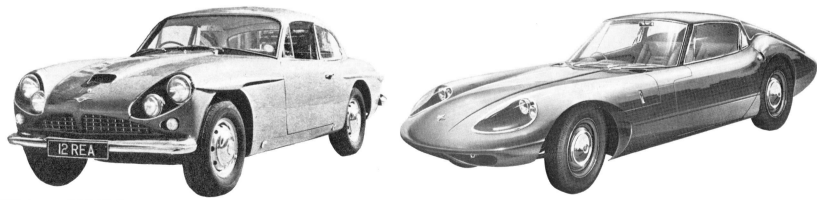

57B Jensen C-V8 Mk II

57C Marcos 1800

58A MG Midget Mk II

58B MG MGB Roadster

58A: **MG** Midget Series GAN Mk II Sports. In line with the development of the Austin-Healey Sprite this new version of the Midget announced in March featured a curved windscreen, push button door handles, fully winding windows with hinged quarter lights, a 3-spoke steering wheel and revised facia layout and instrumentation.

58B: **MG** MGB Sports Roadster continued unchanged, however a fibreglass hardtop became optionally available during the year.

58C: **Morgan** Plus Four Plus GT Fixed Head Coupé. This model which was unveiled in the autumn of 1963, represented something of a break with Morgan tradition, being fitted as it was with a fibreglass, fixed-head coupé body featuring streamlined wings and a narrow, sloping, vertical bar radiator grille with small grilles each side. Engine power was from the Triumph 2138-cc unit.

58C Morgan Plus Four Plus GT

59A Morris Mini Cooper 'S'

59A: **Morris** Mini Cooper 'S 1000' Saloon. One of a number of Cooper variants introduced during the year. This version featured a 970-cc engine which developed 64 bhp at 6500 rpm. 'S 1275' and Mini Cooper (998-cc) models were also available. The Mini-Cooper 'S' (1071-cc engine), introduced during the previous year, was discontinued. Austin versions were also available.

59B: **Morris** Minor 1000. This highly popular range continued with a number of changes, including modified sidelamp units front and rear, improved windscreen wipers, and on two-door models a near-side door lock.

59B Morris Minor 1000

59C Reliant Sabre FH Coupé GT

59C: **Reliant** Sabre FH Coupé GT and Sports models continued unchanged; however, both were discontinued in the late summer.

59D: **Rolls-Royce** Silver Cloud III. A number of modifications were introduced in the early spring, including, on four-door models, the raising of the headlamp fairings to accommodate the 'R-R' monogram. On two-door versions the monogram was incorporated on flat surrounds to the headlamps. A later modification made only to the standard and standard long-wheelbase saloons and the James Young long-wheelbase saloon was the introduction of wider wheel rims.

59D Rolls-Royce Silver Cloud Mk III

60A Rover 2000

60B Singer Gazelle Mk V

60C Sunbeam Rapier Series IV

60A: **Rover** 2000 Saloon. Following a development period of around six years, during which numerous prototypes were made, the Rover Company at last introduced the eagerly awaited production version of the 2000 in the autumn of 1963. This car was, not surprisingly, a huge success both at home and abroad and was given the 'Car of the Year' accolade almost before it was announced. Technical features included a 5 main-bearing, four-cylinder, 1978-cc, ohc engine producing 99 bhp at 5000 rpm, servo assisted disc brakes all round and a very strong body construction which embraced numerous safety features with high levels of interior comfort and space. Maximum speed was in excess of 100 mph.

60B: **Singer** Gazelle Mk V Saloon. Replacement for the Mk IIIC, it featured changes similar to those of the Hillman Minx Series V including a squarer roof line, wider doors and fixed rear quarter lights, a larger windscreen, individual front seats, a redesigned facia and instrument layout, and front disc brakes. Automatic transmission was optionally available.

60C: **Sunbeam** Rapier Series IV Saloon. Superseded the Series IIIA in the autumn of 1963. Changes included a restyled bonnet and front end, reshaped side flashes, modified facia, adjustable steering column, servo-assisted brakes and improvements to the 1592-cc engine which increased the power output. Not available as a convertible.

60D: **Sunbeam** Alpine Series IV. The modified Sports Tourer and GT Hardtop were distinguishable from the discontinued Series III versions mainly by the single horizontal bar radiator grille with central medallion, restyled sidelamp units and rear wings and overriders with rubber inserts. Power output of the engine was increased as for the Series IV Rapier.

60D Sunbeam Alpine Series IV

61A Triumph Spitfire 4 Sports

61A: **Triumph** Spitfire 4 Sports. Continued unchanged although overdrive and a hardtop were now available as optional extras.

61B: **Triumph** 2000 Saloon. Standard-Triumph entered the medium range saloon car market with this attractive Michelotti styled four-door, five-seater which was unveiled in the summer of 1963. Powered by a 90-bhp version of the six-cylinder, 1998-cc engine used on the Vitesse, this model was otherwise completely new and featured a unitary construction body with twin recessed headlamps above a full width horizontal bar grille and a bonnet air scoop, all independent suspension, servo-assisted front brakes and a luxuriously equipped interior. Top speed approximately 95 mph. Price £1087.

61B Triumph 2000

62A Turner 950 Sports

62B TVR Grantura 1800

62C Vanden Plas 1100

62D Vauxhall Viva HA

62A: Turner 950 Sports. The most popular model made by this Wolverhampton based specialist manufacturer, this attractive two-seater was in production between 1957 and 1965 in various forms, powered by the BMC 'A' Series 948-cc engine. Available either in kit form (sold mainly in the UK) or complete. Various other models were also available. Production ceased in 1966.

62B: TVR Grantura Mk III 1800 Sports Coupé. The Lancashire based manufacturer founded in 1959 under the name of Layton Sports Cars Limited, but now operating under the name of Grantura Engineering Limited, introduced their MGB 1798 cc-engined replacement for the MGA-engined Mk III in 1963. Essentially similar in appearance to its predecessor, the '1800' had impressive performance, with a maximum speed approaching 120 mph. Price £1054.

62C: Vanden Plas 1100 Saloon. This luxury variant of the popular front wheel drive 1100 appeared in the autumn of 1963 powered by a twin-carburettor 55-bhp version of the 1098-cc engine unit. Features included a vertical-bar grille, luxury trim, full carpeting, a wooden facia and auxiliary lights. A sunshine roof was optionally available.

62D: Vauxhall Viva HA Saloon. Marking Vauxhall's return to the small saloon car market in the late summer of 1963, after an absence of some years, this two-door model was designed to provide maximum interior accommodation. Features included a four-cylinder, 1057-cc engine developing 44 bhp at 5000 rpm and four-speed all-synchromesh gearbox. Produced initially in Luton and, from July also at Ellesmere Port, the Viva was the first British car to have an acrylic lacquer paint finish. Available in standard and de luxe versions, priced at £527 and £566 respectively. An estate car (Bedford Beagle) conversion by Martin Walter became available in the summer.

63A Vauxhall Victor FB Estate Car

63B Vauxhall VX 4/90

63C Vauxhall Cresta PB Estate Car

63D Wolseley 6/110 Mk II

63A: Vauxhall Victor FB Estate Car. Continued with a number of changes including a larger engine (1595-cc), new clutch, bigger brakes, revised instrument panel layout, restyled radiator grille and additional brightwork. De luxe versions were additionally given a walnut veneer facia, rear arm rests with in-built ashtrays, and distinctive hub caps. Saloon versions were also available.

63B: Vauxhall VX4/90 Saloon. Changes made for 1964 included a larger engine (1595-cc), a new clutch, bigger brakes, revised instrument layout, a walnut veneer facia and full-width parcel shelf.

63C: Vauxhall Cresta PB Estate Car. This variant announced in the winter of 1963 was a conversion by Martin Walter Ltd of Folkestone. A full six-seater—the rear seat had a central arm rest which folded down to give additional passenger room—the model featured a fibreglass roof and a top-hinged rear door. Price £1305. The saloon version continued essentially unchanged. A Velox variant was also available.

63D: Wolseley 6/110 Mk II Saloon replaced the original version in the early spring. New features included a new four-speed gearbox, smaller wheels, self adjusting brakes, revised facia switches, reclining front seats and picnic tables. Overdrive, originally a standard fitment, was now available as an option.

INDEX OF MANUFACTURERS

SUMMARY OF MAJOR BRITISH CAR MAKES
1960–64 (with dates of their existence)

AC	(from 1908)	Lotus	(from 1952)
Alvis	(1920–67)	MG	(from 1924)
Armstrong Siddeley	(1919–60)	Morgan	(from 1910)
Aston Martin	(from 1922)	Morris	(from 1913)
Austin	(from 1906)		
Bentley	(from 1920)	Riley	(1898–1969)
Bristol	(from 1947)	Rolls-Royce	(from 1904)
Daimler	(from 1896)	Rover	(from 1904)
Ford	(from 1911)	Singer	(1905–70)
Hillman	(1907–76)	Standard	(1903–63)
Humber	(1898–76)	Sunbeam	(1953–76)
Jaguar	(from 1932)	Triumph	(from 1953)
Lagonda	(1906–63)	Vauxhall	(from 1903)
		Wolseley	(1911–76)

ABBREVIATIONS

bhp brake horse power
cc cubic centimetres (engine capacity)
mpg miles per gallon
mph miles per hour
ohc overhead camshaft (engine)
ohv overhead valve (engine)
rpm revolutions per minute

ACKNOWLEDGEMENTS

This book was compiled largely from historic source material in the library of the Olyslager Organisation. Grateful thanks are extended to Montagu Motor Museum for the loan of some photographs, to John Weston Hays for his help in locating research material and to Dawn Voller for her valuable assistance in preparing the text.